Poems by JACK PRELUTSKY

My Parents Think I'm Sleeping

Pictures by YOSSI ABOLAFIA

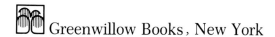 Greenwillow Books, New York

Library of Congress Cataloging in Publication Data

Prelutsky, Jack.
My parents think I'm sleeping.
Summary: A collection of humorous poems about bedtime.
1. Sleep—Juvenile poetry. 2. Children's poetry,
American. [1. Sleep—Poetry. 2. American poetry]
I. Abolafia, Yossi, ill. II. Title.
PS3566.R36M9   1985   811'.54   84-13640
ISBN 0-688-04018-7
ISBN 0-688-04019-5 (lib. bdg.)

FOR AJA AND HER PARENTS

—J.P.

FOR LYNN SMITH

—Y.A.

CONTENTS

MY PARENTS THINK
I'M SLEEPING

My parents think I'm sleeping,
but I'm positively not,
for beneath my pile of covers
I am doing quite a lot.

I am reading poems and stories
(I have got my flashlight lit),
I am playing with the pieces
of my model rocket kit.

I was quiet as my shadow

till the moment they were gone,

then I dove beneath the covers

and I snapped my flashlight on.

So my parents think I'm sleeping,

but that's simply their mistake,

I have got them fooled completely,

I am really wide-awake.

TONIGHT IS IMPOSSIBLY NOISY

Tonight is impossibly noisy,
it's filled with a horrible sound,
as if dozens of ogres and tigers
are stuck on a merry-go-round.

It sounds like a monkey battalion

is dancing on needles and pins,

or an out-of-tune elephant orchestra

is sawing on steel violins.

Tonight is impossibly noisy,

the air's full of screeches and roars,

it sounds as if pigs are stampeding,

pursued by enraged dinosaurs.

It sounds like a poltergeist army
is holding a midnight parade,
but it's only the alley cat chorus
in a brassy backyard serenade.

THE CLOUDS I WATCHED THIS AFTERNOON

The clouds I watched this afternoon
were flocks of silent sheep,
but now they've turned to smoky wolves
that watch *me* while I sleep.

All night they prowl before the moon,
till morning, when I rise,
then once again white fleecy sheep
will float across the skies.

NIGHT IS HERE

Night is here, and night is there,
and night is all around,
I feel its presence everywhere,
and yet it makes no sound.

And so it's time to close my eyes
and dream the night away,
until the sun lights up the skies,
and welcomes back the day.

A SPOOKY SORT
OF SHADOW

There's a spooky sort of shadow
dancing weirdly on the wall,
it's a creature that
I've never seen before,
it's creepy, and it's eerie,
and so positively tall,
that it stretches from
the ceiling to the floor.

Its mouth is full of needles,

and it has a giant eye,

and it's moving

in a hungry sort of way,

it surely could destroy me

if it only cared to try,

so I hope it's had enough

to eat today.

That shadow makes me nervous,

I don't dare to close my eyes,

I'm afraid I may be eaten,

head and all—

if I fall asleep tonight,

I'll be taken by surprise

by that shadow dancing

on my bedroom wall.

WHAT HAPPENS
TO THE COLORS?

What happens to the colors
when night replaces day?
What turns the wrens to ravens,
the trees to shades of gray?

Who paints away the garden
when the sky's a sea of ink?
Who robs the sleeping flowers
of their purple and their pink?

What makes the midnight clover
quiver black upon the lawn?
What happens to the colors?
What brings them back at dawn?

I HAVE BEEN IN BED
FOR HOURS

I have been in bed for hours,
but I'm sure I'm wide-awake,
for my head is filled with visions
of a forest by a lake.

I hear frogs and crickets calling,

I'm aware of fireflies,

I can see the moon reflected

in an owl's unblinking eyes.

I tiptoe very softly

past a hive of drowsy bees,

high above, a cloud meanders,

tiny stars shine through the trees.

I sit beside the water

as a silent swan glides by,

I climb a breezy hilltop,

where I almost touch the sky.

I watch the fishes splashing

in a clear and crystal stream,

it's a very lovely forest,

far too real to be a dream.

CHOCOLATE CAKE

I am lying in the darkness
with a smile upon my face,
as I'm thinking of my stomach,
which has got an empty space,
and that corner of the kitchen
with the piece of chocolate cake
I have got to get my hands on
for my empty stomach's sake.

When my parents both are sleeping

(I can tell by Father's snore),

I will sneak out of my bedroom,

I will tiptoe past their door,

I will slip into the kitchen

without any noise or light,

and if I'm really careful,

I will have that cake tonight.

RAIN

I was having trouble sleeping
when I heard the pleasant sound
of raindrops softly falling
on the rooftop and the ground.

I hurried to the window
just to watch them as they fell,
they filled the night with sparkles,
and a fresh and lovely smell.

I started feeling sleepy
so I climbed back into bed,
and fell asleep while listening
to the raindrops overhead.

IT IS SO STILL

It is so still, so still tonight,
there is no sound at all,
no tapping on a windowpane,
no footsteps in the hall,

no barking dog or screeching cat,

no mouse beneath my bed,

no rustle of a windy leaf,

no raindrops overhead.

I lie beneath my covers

with my pillow to my ear,

and my breathing and my heartbeat

are the only sounds I hear.

IF IT WAS SUNLIGHT SHINING

If it was sunlight shining,
I'd know that it was day,
I'd gobble down my breakfast,
then hurry out to play.

If it was sunlight shining,

I would not be indoors,

I'd race around the garden,

I'd fill the air with roars.

If it was sunlight shining,

I'd be a chimpanzee,

I'd run, I'd jump, I'd tumble,

I'd clamber up a tree.

But it is moonlight shining,
my eyes are getting red,
my head is full of cobwebs,
and I am off to bed.

WHEN I'M VERY NEARLY SLEEPING

When I'm very nearly sleeping
in the middle of the night,
and I hear the furtive creeping
of a thing that likes to bite,
you may be completely certain
that I haven't any fear,
though when it is on the curtain,
how I wish it were not here.

When I sense the creature perching

on my pillow underneath,

and suspect that it is searching

for a spot to sink its teeth,

when I'm sure I feel it flitting

but an inch above my head,

I am glad a lamp is sitting

on the table by my bed.

A MILLION CANDLES

A million candles fill the night,
they glister in the dark,
and though by day they hide their glow,
now each displays its spark.

Amidst them all, there is one light
that has a special shine,
and that's the one whose name I know . . .
I think that it knows mine.

I'M AWAKE!
I'M AWAKE!

I'm awake! I'm awake!
I cannot shut my eyes,
I'm unable to sleep,
though I've made many tries,

I'm sure I've explored
every inch of my bed,
my body's exhausted,
and so is my head.

I wiggle, I fidget,

I tumble, I twist,

I pound my poor pillow

with fist after fist,

I stopped counting sheep
when I reached ninety-three.
I'm awake! I'm awake!
I cannot fall asleeeeeeeeee